PIT BOSS WOOD PELLET GRILL & SMOKER COOKBOOK

VEGETABLES

Mark Eastwood

TABLE OF CONTENTS

Food Grade Wood Pellets For Smoking And Grilling 10

The Best Wood Pellets For Smoking And Grilling 12

Why Should I Replace My Grill With A Pellet Grill? 14

How To Clean A Pit Boss 22

How To Clean A Pellet Grill 25

1. Grilled Baby Carrots And Fennel With Romesco 36
2. Grilled Hummus 38
3. Smoked Apple Cider 41
4. Pit Bossed Smoked Mushrooms 43
5. Roasted Tomatoes 45
6. Burnt Orange Julep Cocktail 47
7. Blackberry Bourbon Smash 50
8. Grilled Watermelon 53
9. SMOKED SHREDDED BRUSSELS SPROUT SALAD 55
10. SMOKED PICO DE GALLO 58
11. Grilled Winter Chop Salad 60
12. Grilled Broccoli Rabe 63
13. Grilled Baby Carrots And Fennel With Romesco 65
14. Smoked Cold Brew Coffee 67
15. Grilled Corn On The Cob With Parmesan And Garlic 70
16. Salt Crusted Baked Potatoes 72
17. Grilled Salmon w/ Honey Sriracha Lime Glaze 74
18. Grilled Winter Chop Salad 75

19.	Lemon & Garlic Asparagus	78
20.	Crab Stuffed Mushrooms	80
21.	Lemon-Garlic Green Beans	82
22.	Spinach Artichoke Chicken Grilled Cheese	84
23.	Mexican Street Corn Salad	86
24.	Brussels Sprout Slaw With Apple Butter Dressing	88
25.	Green Chile Mashed Potatoes	91
26.	Smoked Scalloped Potatoes	93
27.	Southern Green Beans	95
28.	Gluten Free Mashed Potato Cakes	97
29.	Chili Verde Sauce	100
30.	Smoked Paprika Cauliflower	102
31.	Roasted Sweet Potato Steak Fries	103
32.	Smoked Cabbage	105
33.	Eggplant	106
34.	Grilled Broccoli Rabe	107
35.	Smoked Pumpkin Soup	109
36.	Baked Deep Dish Supreme Pizza	112
37.	Bacon Onion Ring	114
38.	Roasted Peach Salsa	116
39.	Roasted Green Beans With Bacon	119

THE FUNDAMENTALS OF WOOD PELLET GRILLING AND SMOKING

Wood pellets are the fuel source of pellet grills and smokers. Pit Boss Grills hardwood pellets are made from 100% all-natural hardwood that is dried and ground into sawdust. The dust is then pressurized at extreme heat to create the compact pellets that are coated and held together with the wood's natural lignin. Wood pellets are also known as the easiest fuel to use. They produce less than 1% of ash, so an entire 40lb bag of pellets will only turn into ½ cup of ash, which makes clean up a breeze. They also provide immense flavor without needing to think about babysitting the air to fuel ratios like wood chips or chunks.

Food Grade Wood Pellets For Smoking And Grilling

It's important to note that there are food grade pellets and non-food grade or heating pellets. Heating pellets (or pellets used in wood-burning stoves) can be made from wood that isn't meant for smoking meat. Woods like pine or spruce can ruin the flavor of your food. Who wants their brisket tasting like a car air freshener anyway? Heating pellets may also contain glues or other chemicals as binders, which is not only bad for flavor but terrible for your health as well.

What Are Wood Pellets And How Are They Made?

Food grade wood pellets, on the other hand, are made purely from hardwood and lack any chemical binders or glues. Since food consumption is the priority they are made with the same standards and practices as any other food grade product, meaning sanitation and health are at the forefront of production and packaging concerns.

Since food-grade wood pellets are made specifically for cooking, certain hardwoods are chosen due to the flavor and aroma they produce when smoking. We'll get into which flavors are produced and how they pair with certain foods a little later.

Food Grade Hardwood Pellets Include:

- Mesquite
- Hickory
- Cherry
- Pecan
- Apple
- Oak
- Alder

Wood Pellets And The Environment

You might be thinking to yourself:

- "Is all that wood-burning good for the environment?"
- "What about all those trees?"

- "Are wood pellets better and more efficient than other fuel sources?"

These are fantastic questions and we're glad you asked. Wood pellets are sourced from tree farms (which replace the trees they process), storm-damaged trees, and trees at the end of their lifecycle in hardwood forests across the United States:

Low CO2 Production

Including manufacturing and transportation costs, it is estimated that burning wood pellets produces 34g carbon dioxide per KiloWatt Hour of heat produced (g/kWh). Compare that with 211 grams for gas and 64 for wood chips. "The Carbon Balance of Woodfuel", Northern Woodhead, 2010".

The Best Wood Pellets For Smoking And Grilling

If you're going to smoke or grill a meal on a wood pellet grill, it's best to know which type of hardwood to use to enhance the flavor of your food.

- Should you use a flavored or blended pellet?
- Which flavors go best with different types of food?

These are great questions to ask when choosing wood pellets. You also want to be sure to pick a quality brand of pellets as well. A cheaply made brand can not only ruin your food but can wreak havoc on your pellet grill as well. For this reason, we recommend using Pit Boss Grills Wood Pellets on a Pit Boss Pellet Grill. Since we know where they came from, we know they will work fine on our products. If you don't own a Pit Boss Grill, feel free to use them on other pellet grills as we stand firmly behind our wood pellets.

Wood Pellet Flavors

Competition Blend: Sweet and smoky with an aromatic tang. A premium blend of cherry, hickory, and maple hardwoods. Masterfully craft sweet, savory aroma combined with a soft fruity undertone for your beef, pork, chicken, seafood, desserts, fruits, or veggies.

Mesquite: Strong aroma with a tangy and spicy flavor. The perfect level of bold taste to compliment your Tex-Mex cuisine.

Hickory: Rich with a smoky bacon-like flavor. Highly recommended for roasts and smoking your favorite meats.

Apple: Smokey with a mild sweetness flavor. Highly recommended for baking and pork.

Classic: A bold southern blend of pecan, hickory, and mesquite wood. Full-bodied, robust flavor that will bring out the best in chicken, pork, seafood, or vegetables.

Charcoal Blend: A bold aroma of oak hardwood with the robust, classic taste of smoky charcoal. The perfect choice for uniting the greatest flavors in outdoor cooking. Use this powerhouse blend to enrich the mouthwatering flavors of beef, pork, poultry, or game.

What Is A Pellet Grill?

Pellet grills are outdoor cookers that combine elements of smokers, charcoal grills, gas grills, and ovens. They use 100% all-natural food-grade hardwood pellets. Hardwood pellets are the fuel source that allows Country Smokers to provide indirect heat (meaning the food isn't cooked directly over the flame, it is cooked by the radiant heat that circulates throughout the grill, like an oven).

Why Should I Replace My Grill With A Pellet Grill?

Three reasons: flavor, convenience, and versatility.

1. Flavor

Through the burning of hardwood pellets, everything you cook gets infused with a plank of real wood, smoky flavor. The fan inside the grill forces heat and smoke to circulate over the food while the lid is closed. All that savory wood flavor and aroma gets infused into the food as it cooks. The result is a delicious smoke flavor that enhances but doesn't overwhelm, the flavor of the food.

2. Convenience

Pellet grills are super easy to use. Plug it in, fill the hopper with pellets, turn it on, set your temperature, and let it cook. Come back when the food looks and feels done.

Versatility

Anything you can cook on a charcoal or gas grill, you can cook on a pellet grill (and then some). Whether you're craving ribs, burgers, steaks, brisket, pulled pork, pies, pizza - your options are truly endless.

What Are Wood Pellets?

Wood pellets are the fuel source of pellet grills and smokers. Louisiana Grills® hardwood pellets are made from 100% all-natural hardwood that is dried and ground into sawdust. The dust is then pressurized at extreme heat to create the compact pellets that are coated and held together with the wood's natural lignin. Wood pellets are also known as the easiest fuel to use. They produce less than 1% of ash, so an entire 40lb bag of pellets will only turn into ½ cup of ash, which makes clean up a breeze. The wood pellets also provide immense flavor, and there is no need to worry about monitoring the air to fuel ratio like you would with wood chips or chunks.

Seasoning Your Pellet Grill

I recommend seasoning or breaking in, your pellet grill before you cook. Seasoning your grill will remove any kind of solvents or impurities on the grill. This also helps add the "smoke" or "grilled" flavor since you are lining the inside of your grill with wood smoke (seasoning process is similar to that of a Dutch oven). To season your pellet grill:

- Fill the pellet hopper with pellets.
- Plug your grill into a power source.
- Make sure the flame deflector is in place over the firepot.
- Flip the power switch to the ON position.
- Use the arrows to set the temperature to 400°F and let smoke for at least 1 hour.

You can also season your grill grates by simply rubbing them with cooking oil and placing them in the grill so they can be seasoned while the inside of your grill is running. It might take several minutes for the pellets to drop into the firepot. Make sure the unit lights. If the unit does not light, try turning the unit off and back on to restart the ignitor.

If there is a failure with your auto ignitor, you can follow these steps to manually light your pellet grill:

- Make sure the firepot is empty and not burning.
- Pour ½ cup pellets into the firepot.
- Squirt approximately 2 tablespoons of alcohol gel into the firepot.
- Carefully, light with a match.

- Let the pellets burn for 4-5 minutes, flip the switch to ON.
- Set the thermostat to the desired temperature.

REMINDER: Only use 100% food-grade pellets with your pellet grill. Using non approved hardwood barbecue pellets will void your warranty. Also, avoid getting pellets wet. Wet pellets will swell and fall apart which could clog the auger.

Pit Boss Grills Pellet Flavors Guide

We manufacture the perfect wood pellet flavors for any type of food you can cook on a pellet grill or smoker. The following are flavors we recommend for each type but feel free to experiment on your own:

1. Beef: Charcoal, Georgia Pecan, Mesquite, Competition Blend, Hickory, Classic Blend.

2. Poultry: Competition Blend, Mesquite, Classic Blend, Hickory, Apple, Fruit, Charcoal.

3. Pork: Competition Blend, Mesquite, Classic Blend, Hickory, Apple, Fruit, Charcoal.

4. Seafood: Competition Blend, Apple, Fruit

5. Veggies: Competition Blend, Apple, Hickory, Fruit

Unmatched Wood Pellet Flavor And Quality

Pit Boss Grills makes wood pellets that set the standard for flavor and quality in the pellet grill industry. We make our wood pellets with the highest quality food-grade hardwood, free of artificial flavors, spray scents, glues, or chemicals. Burn hotter and cleaner. Our pellets are easy to use, great-tasting, and all-natural, forcing the natural juices in the wood to bind the pellets together.

Pit Boss P Setting – What Is It And How/When To Adjust It?

If you own an older Pit Boss pellet grill or a current Pit Boss Tailgater, Renegade, or the Scout portable pellet grill you may be able to adjust the P-Setting. But what the heck is the P-Setting and why should you want to learn when and how to change it anyway!? Well, the P-Setting is an abbreviation of the Pause Setting. Essentially, the P-Setting dictates the timed gap between turning the pellet feed auger on to feed in fresh grill pellets into the firepot to maintain the set temperature. Through adjustment of the P-Setting, you may be able to get your Pit Boss to more accurately hold its set temperature and/or produce more smoke when dsired.

Introduction To The Pit Boss P-Setting

As stated above the P-Setting stands for Pause Setting. I also stated above that any modern Pit Boss on the D2 platform doesn't have a P-Setting button on the control panel. Well, just to make things a bit more complicated not every earlier generation Pit

Boss grill controller has the P-Setting button either. If your controller does have this button it will be to the right of the digital readout display, likely with a small 'call service' sticker over the top.

To access the P-Setting button you will need to take that sticker off. The official video below from Pit Boss discusses the P-Setting button in more detail and when you would want to adjust the auger pause settings.

When/How To Adjust The Pit Boss's P-Setting

As stated in Pit Boss's official video above on when/how to adjust the grills P-Setting, if you are using the grill in an area/time of year with an extremely cold/warm climate, adjustments to the P-Setting may pay dividends in terms of more accurate cooking experience. If your Pit Boss pellet grill is operating far below or far above the set temperature on the dial (more than 25 degrees) then you should consider adjusting the P-Setting where possible.

If the pellet grill is running more than the set temperature you adjust the P-Setting up to a higher number. If the pellet grill is running significantly below your set temperature you adjust the P-Setting down to a lower number. Unless you have adjusted the P-Setting before, it's only recommended jumping 1 number at a time. Once you are more familiar with how changing the P-Setting alters the performance of your pellet grill you may have a preferred specific number for a specific outside temperature.

However, even though in the official Pit Boss video above a screwdriver is used I wouldn't do that. After all its turned on when you are adjusting the P-Setting with 110V flowing through it. I would personally use a wooden toothpick or something similar.

Pit Boss Owners Video On P-Setting Adjustments

While the official Pit Boss video above on adjusting the P-Setting is better than nothing, I don't think it goes into enough detail on the matter. Therefore, I wanted to include in this post the video below. I believe it does a far better job of explaining the circumstances and scenarios of when to change the P-Setting on a Pit Boss pellet grill.

Risks With Using A High Number P-Setting

Something which is mentioned in the video above which is very important to pay attention to is the risks of using a high number P-Setting, say the maximum of 9 during windy conditions. As new fuel is fed into the firepot very infrequently, there is a risk that as the wind picks up it could extinguish the smoldering pellets altogether.

However, the pellet grill controller will not know the fire has gone out, so it will keep feeding in wood pellets. In that scenario, you cannot just turn the pellet grill off and on again. There will be a significant volume of wood pellets in the firepot. If you just turn the pellet grill on again it will likely lead to a smoke explosion. So if the pellet grill fire does go out completely you will need to clean out the burn pot of pellets before can start the grill up again. Its scenarios such as this which make the quick ash/pellet removal feature on Camp Chefs Woodwind and SmokePro pellet grills very useful indeed.

Pit Boss P-Setting Examples/Results

At the end of the above video, some useful examples are given in terms of P-Settings at certain outside temperatures which they found to work well. For instance, with a 70 degree outside temperature and no wind, they found that the factory P-Setting on their Pit Boss pellet grill of 4 produces a temperature of between 150-160 degrees while on the smoke setting. However, compare that to the example of smoking brisket on a cold winter evening. In that scenario, they found that a P-Setting of 0 was required to achieve a constant temperature of 160 degrees.

MAINTENANCE

How To Clean A Pit Boss

Cleaning Tips

1. When to clean your grill

- I clean mine every 3-5 cooks, more often if I'm cooking higher fat foods

2. Steps to clean your Pit Boss

- Make sure the grill is cool and unplugged
- Open Pellet hopper lid, place 5-gallon bucket under the back pellet door, and drain pellets into a bucket. Save for re-use

3. Open Pit Boss lid and using a grill brush scrub the top of the grates

- Turn grates over and scrub the underside (which is now the top) of the grates
- BE CAREFUL not to hit the temperature probe with the grates while turning them over

4. Remove the grates and set aside

5. Assess the amount of soot or particulate on the inside of the barrel

- Lightly scrape with the paint tool

- Use the paint tool to get around the edges of the grill and into the corners

Push All Crumbs Into The Bottom Of The Barrel

- Remove the drip tray, remove the foil or foil liners, and asses for any stuck-on food/debris
- Brush off the heat shield and remove
- Brush off lower heat shield and remove *(only if very deep cleaning, will need a screwdriver)*
- Check all edges and corners of the grill for debris and scrape into the lower barrel
- Check the drip trough for any debris and scrape into the grease bucket
- Reline drip tray with new liners or foil
- Once all cleaning from top to bottom has been done, plug in the Vacuum
- Vacuum out the entire inside of the grill including the ledges and corners
- Vacuum out the firepot and a little bit into the auger
- Vacuum out the hopper to remove any excess sawdust, vacuum out down into the auger as well
- Verify inside the barrel is clean and all parts/bolts are tight and everything is in working order

- Rebuild the grill from the bottom up starting with the lower heat shield, upper heat shield, drip tray with fresh liners or foil, bottom grate, and top grate
- Refill pellet hopper with pellets
- Using the Pit Boss Grill cleaner, spray all sides as heavy as needed, allow to soak for 1 minute, and wipe down the grill from top to bottom. Spot clean again if heavier cleaning is needed. I wipe down the sides of the grill and legs as well
- Remove the grease bucket and change out the foil liner and clean the bucket if needed
- Plug grill in (good time to check the cord), Turn on the grill, turn to 200 degrees and ignite. Once the grill reaches 200 degrees, verify operation and place the grill back into shutdown mode
- You can skip this part and wait until your next cook to do it Grill Maintenance

Cleaning your grill regularly is very important in maintaining a functioning grill. We recommend cleaning the grill after every 2-3 cooks. However, you may need to clean it out more often when cooking greasier foods or after a long cook.

1. Spray the grill grate and inside of the chimney with an all-natural degreaser/cleaner.

2. Remove and clean both sides of the grill grates.

3. Dispose of old foil or drip tray liners.

4. Remove the drip tray and the heat baffle.

5. Vacuum the inside of the grill and the firepot thoroughly.

7. Spray the inside and outside of the grill with the all-natural degreaser/cleaner and allow to soak for several minutes before wiping clean with a paper towel or cleaning cloth.

8. Last, reinsert all components including the heat baffle, drip try, drip tray liners/foil, new bucket liners, and the grill grates and you are set!

How To Clean A Pellet Grill

As an avid BBQer, my grill is often in need of a good cleaning. To be a BBQ hero and cook delicious food for the people you love, you need to know how to clean a pellet grill. Today, I'm sharing all my tips and tricks for how to deep clean a grill and get it ready for that next big cookout.

Deep Cleaning Your Grill

Today, we're talking all about getting your pellet smoker back in pristine shape. After smoking delicious food all week, your grill is likely in need of a little love. My smoker of choice is my Camp Chef SmokePro SGX, but this post applies to any smoker that you have and the tools we are using work all across the board. No matter what is on your back patio, these tips and tricks can help you figure out the best way to clean your grill.

Best Way To Clean A Pellet Grill

Let's get cleaning! I always recommend beginning at the top and working your way to the bottom.

1. **Clean The Lid:** Use a putty knife and a nylon scrubber to scrape the buildup on the lid. These two items are must-haves when cleaning all the carbon and residue from your grill.

2. **Empty It:** Remove most of the components in your grill, including the grates, drip pan, and deflector plate. Use your putty knife and scrubber to rub them down and get that extra gunk off.

Scrape Everything! Scrape The Inside Of The Barrel: Rub your putty knife on all the lips and edges as well. Make sure you hit the area in the back where the chimney is attached to the barrel because there will a lot of buildup in there. Also, spend plenty of time cleaning the chimney. If you have a drip tray that has vents in it, use the corner of your putty knife to get these nice and clear so none of them are blocked.hand with putty knife scraping barrel of a pellet grill

Clean The Grates: If you have grates that break apart into smaller pieces, you can wash them in the dishwasher. If your grill does not have grates you can put in the dishwasher, use a nylon scrub brush (on cold grates only!), or balled up tin foil between a pair of tongs (for hot grates) to scrape them clean. Check out more details on cleaning grill grates in the next paragraph.

Don't forget the thermometer and grease chute! Use a paper towel to clean the thermometer inside your grill. This is what dictates how frequently your grill feed pellets, how hot your grill gets, and it can impact temp swings. Also, make sure you thoroughly clean the grease chute. It connects the drip tray to the grease bucket. Grease spillage can occur if this gets blocked, and it can set you up for a grease fire, so use your putty knife to get this nice and clean.

Vacuum Out All The Gunk: Once you've scraped off all the residue in your grill, grab a wet/dry vacuum to suck out everything that you've worked loose.

Clean The Exterior: I use a degreaser and Windex to get my smoker sparkling clean. If your grill is stainless steel, use a stainless steel wipe or spray to get your shine on! You can also use a thin oil like vegetable oil to wipe down the exterior of your grill and it conditions everything and makes it look brand new.

Reassemble: Put your grill back together and you're ready to get smoking again!

How To Clean Grill Grates

Cleaning grates on your pellet grill is a bit tricky, but here are some tips to get them clean fast.

Use Appropriate Cleaning Products: The grill grates on my Camp Chef SGX come off, and I put them in the dishwasher to get all the baked-on gunk off. If yours don't come off in small enough sections for your dishwasher, use a nylon scrub brush for cold grates, or balled up tin foil between a pair of tongs for hot grates. Both of these can get into the grooves and knock off the bigger pieces of burnt-on gunk.

Degreaser Works Wonders: I can fit my grates in my dishwasher, so I wash mine through with a degreaser. You can also use a spray degreaser to break down the buildup. You can also remove the grates and soak them in a plastic bin or your bathtub with blue dish soap.

Avoid Using Water Inside Your Smoker: Almost all smokers have metal components inside them that can rust. Avoid this and only use water once you remove the grates.

Avoid abrasive grill brushes! Do not use the grill brushes with wire bristles. They can damage the protective coating on your grates and rust them out. These bristles may also flake off, and you run the risk of ingesting them and getting seriously hurt.

Clean pellet grill on a patio

Recipes For Your Clean Pellet Grill

Once your pellet smoker is clean, let's get it good and dirty again with these delicious smoked recipes:

- Texas Style Smoked Beef Brisket
- Smoked Mac and Cheese
- Smoked Tri-Tip

Pit Boss Grill Troubleshooting Guide – 10 Problem And Solution

Pit Boss grills are now hot cake in the markets. If we compare any sort of with Pit Boss Grill is high tech, relying on Multiple parts that work in the mixture to create a set it and forget it BBQ experience Pit Boss propagates flourished grills and barbecues for cooking. The apparatus mainly used for grilling, smoking the barbecue. This is featured with automatic start, electronic temperature control, etc. I am going to talk about 10 Pit Boss grill troubleshooting, error/problem including solution too. Like all pellet grills, the Pit Boss grill has some limitations and lackings. The grill not flaming up, pellets not founding into the fire pit, crack with declining temperature. All the problems can be resolved by a troubleshooting guide. The troubleshooting guide is given below:

10 Pit Boss Grill Troubleshooting – Problem And Solution

1. Unusual Heat Oscillation

The most common problem of the Pit Boss grill is its unusual heat swings. Sometimes it takes a long time to heat up. Depending on the outside temperature the grill takes 5 or 10 minutes to heat up.

Solution

When you use your Pit Boss for the first time it will take approximately 7 minutes. We all know that perfectly cooked or smoked food depends on the right heat or temperature. It is pretty annoying that when the set temperature starts oscillating on your Pit Boss grill. You might treat it as a problem but some oscillation is quite normal. According to Pit Boss, during your cooking, you will experience that temperature oscillates of about 20 degrees.

If you firing up your grill in all seasons then you can expect the temperature to swings beyond the 20-degree range. To solve this problem you have to think about the wood pellets you are using. Are they perfect for Pit Boss pellets or are you storing them correctly and so on. If the pellets are okay then take a look at the fire pot and other parts to analyze their condition. You need to clean and replace the Pit Boss. If you see everything is fine but the temperature is still swinging then it could be a temperature problem. So it is not a big deal for you in using the Pit Boss grill.

2. Mitigated Fire

Many users complain about Pit Boss for mitigating fire. This problem is almost the same as temperature swings. In the same way, you need to clean and replace the firepot because it is unable to maintain the fire. There need much ash or deterioration inside the firepot, which makes airflow obstruction and causing air to die.

Solution

Pit Boss grill has an induction fan. This fan provides oxygen to keep going its work and if it doesn't the fire will mitigate. If you notice any damage in any parts you should replace it away.

To have a long-lasting, clean the grill after every use, clean the ash after two or three sessions and do a complete cleaning at least two or three times a year. If the fan is not running and the fire mitigating problem is not solved then you can choose different pellets to use and store them correctly to conserve their quality. Because Better quality pellets will ensure that the grill is not burning too much. So, this problem can be solved if you follow this.

3. Pellets Not Passing

You don't have to stand beside the grill and keep adding pellets constantly because the Pit Boss grill comes with an automated auger and hopper that can do the work for you. But many grilling lover persons face this problem that the pellets not moving from the hopper to the firepot.

Solution

In this case, you need to take out your toolbox and open up some part of the grill, especially the hopper side. If you see the main problem is in the motor then you need to repair or replace it or if it's a jam, you'll simply need to clear it up. Then you have to assemble it and you can use the grill happily.

4. Firepot Not Flaming

The Pit Boss grill user allegations that the fire is not flaming up in the pot. This could be happening for many reasons. Like:

- ❖ The fire pot is not found any pallets to burn.
- ❖ The igniter or hot rod is crashing.
- ❖ Excessive ash

Solution

If the igniter or the fan is crashing in this case you have to repair it if you can. If you are unable to do it then you can replace the hot rod with better stainless steel components which would be more long-lasting.

5. Grill Not Powering On

Charcoal or gas grill does not require power to on but Pit Boss grill requires power to on. It is a common and simple problem for the user. Ultimate components like induction fan and auger motor need electricity to work and make your BBQ alluring.

Solution

This problem can be solved if you settle or replace firmly fix components that are creating the problem. Sometimes the grill need not power on because of a tripped GFCI, a blown fuse, or a bad power outlet.

6. The Grills Fan Is Not Turning On

It is a common problem that the induction is not working. It happens for several reasons. Firstly, this can happen for the lack of power from the controller to the orange wires. Lastly, similar obstructions can restrain the fan from spinning.

Solution

The induction fan is the most essential component in the grill. If it doesn't work then you will be unable to do anything on your grill. If you notice the fan is not working due to some obstructions, then you can withdraw it manually and the fan should start again. This way the induction fan will do its work.

7. The Grill Is Not Smoking

It is a vital complaint about Pit Boss Grill that sometimes the grill is not smoking. The main purpose of a grill is to smoke. But when the grill halt to smoke then it turns into a major problem.

Solution

High Temperature is the main cause of the impediment of smoking. The wood pellets are producing less smoke. In this case, you should use hardwood pellets. Softwood pallets are unable to produce smoke. You should check for a smoke every three to five minutes.

8. The Fire Goes Out Frequently

Another annoying problem with the Pit Boss grill is the fire is going out in the middle of cooking. This problem is the root of many other problems like temperature swings, excessive ash, etc.

Solution

Dump pallets are the main cause of this problem. So you should keep the pellets in the right place and restore them accurately. If you can prevent this then it would be able to maintain a fire.

9. Takes Too Much To Cook

The user complaints about this model that it takes too much time for cooking. It happens to lots of problems.

Solution

This problem is related to temperature swings and a fire going out. When the fire is going out in the middle of cooking then temperature swings and then it takes too much time to cook.

1. GRILLED BABY CARROTS AND FENNEL WITH ROMESCO

Prep Time : 15 Minutes

Cook Time : 45 Minutes

Pellets : Oak

Smoked romesco sauce on top of this roasted trio of baby carrots, fingerling potatoes, and fennel bulbs will make you sing Hallelujah thanks to it intensely fresh and tangy wood-fired flavor.

How Many People Are You Serving? 8

Ingredients

- 1 Pound slender rainbow carrots or regular carrots with tops on
- 2 fennel bulbs, stalks, and cores removed and halved
- 1 pound fingerling potatoes, washed and halved lengthwise
- 1/4 cup olive oil
- kosher salt
- 1 Tablespoon thyme or rosemary leaves

Steps

1. When ready to cook, set Pit Boss temperature to 500°F and preheat, lid closed for 15 minutes. Grill: 500°

2. Trim the carrot tops to 1 inch. Peel the carrots and halve any larger ones so they are all about 1/2 inch thick. Cut the fennel bulbs lengthwise into 1/2 inch thick slices. Place the carrots, fennel, and potato slices in a large mixing bowl. Drizzle with olive oil and a generous teaspoon of salt. Toss to coat the vegetables evenly with the oil.

3. Transfer the vegetables to a sheet pan. Nestle a few sprigs of herbs into the vegetables as well.

4. Place the pan directly on the grill grate and cook, stirring occasionally until the vegetables are browned and softened, about 35 to 45 minutes. Allow to cool and serve with the Smoked Romesco Sauce. Enjoy! Grill: 500°

2. GRILLED HUMMUS

Prep Time : 20 Minutes

Cook Time : 40 Minutes

Pellets : Pecan

Smoke-infused hummus is a smooth & healthy side dip that's great with veggies or chips.

How Many People Are You Serving? 4

Ingredients

- ❖ 1 Head garlic
- ❖ As Needed extra-virgin olive oil
- ❖ 2 small lemons
- ❖ 1 Can Chickpeas
- ❖ 3/2 Tablespoon tahini
- ❖ 1/4 cup extra-virgin olive oil
- ❖ As Needed salt
- ❖ As Needed pepper
- ❖ As Needed Pita Bread

Steps

1. When ready to cook, set the Pit Boss to 375°F (180 C) and preheat, lid closed for 15 minutes. Grill: 375°

2. Slice the top off of the garlic, until garlic cloves are exposed. Pour a small amount of olive oil over the top; wrap in foil. Place wrapped garlic head on the grill grate. Grill for 30 minutes. Add halved lemons, after 30 minutes, and cook all ingredients for an additional 10 minutes. Grill: 375°

3. Drain half of the chickpea juice; reserve the rest for the dip. Place chickpeas in a blender. Add Tahini paste.

4. Remove garlic and lemons from grill; allow to cool slightly.

5. Unwrap garlic and squeeze out 6 to 8 cloves into the blender. Squeeze 2 halves of lemons into the blender, being careful to not allow seeds to fall in.

6. Add 1/4 cup (100 mL) of olive oil to the blender. Pulse all ingredients until smooth. Add salt and pepper to taste. Additionally, paprika or cumin can be added.

7. Toast pita bread and serve with hummus.

3. SMOKED APPLE CIDER

Prep Time : 5 Minutes

Cook Time : 30 Minutes

Pellets : Apple

A fall classic gets an infusion smoky flavor in our smoked apple cider recipe. Set grill to smoke setting, then combine cider, a cinnamon stick, star anise, clove, lemon, and orange peel in a shallow baking dish and place directly on the grill grate for 30 minutes.

How Many People Are You Serving? 2

Ingredients

- 32 Ounce apple cider
- 2 cinnamon sticks
- 4 whole cloves
- 3-star anise
- 2 Pieces orange peel
- 2 Pieces lemon peel

Steps

1. When ready to cook, set Pit Boss temperature to 225°F and preheat, lid closed for 15 minutes. For optimal flavor, use Super Smoke if available. Grill: 225°

2. Combine the cider, cinnamon stick, star anise, clove, lemon, and orange peel in a shallow baking dish.

3. Place directly on the grill grate and smoke for 30 minutes. Remove from grill, strain, and transfer to four mugs. Grill: 225°

4. Finish with a slice of apple and a cinnamon stick to serve. Enjoy!

4. PIT BOSSED SMOKED MUSHROOMS

Prep Time : 15 Minutes

Cook Time : 45 Minutes

Pellets : Apple

This tasty side dish just might steal the show. Mushrooms require little prep time and absorb that rich, hardwood smoke flavor. Toss them into any recipe that calls for mushrooms, add a hint of smoke, and an earthy depth to your dish.

How Many People Are You Serving? 4

Ingredients

- 4 Cup Baby Portobello, whole, cleaned
- 1 Tablespoon canola oil
- 1 teaspoon onion powder

- ❖ 1 teaspoon granulated garlic
- ❖ 1 teaspoon salt
- ❖ 1 Teaspoon pepper

Steps

1. Combine all the ingredients in a mixing bowl.

2. When ready to cook, set temperature to 180°F and place mushrooms directly on the grill, and smoke for 30 minutes. Grill: 180°

3. Increase the grill temperature to High and finish cooking mushrooms, about 15 minutes longer. Serve warm.

5. ROASTED TOMATOES

Prep Time : 5 Minutes

Cook Time : 3 Hours

Pellets : Alder

For a perfectly balanced meal, accompany your main meat event with this delicious, colorful, & healthy side dish.

How Many People Are You Serving? 2

Ingredients

- ❖ 3 large ripe tomatoes

- 1/2 Tablespoon kosher salt
- 1 teaspoon coarse ground black pepper
- 1/4 teaspoon sugar
- 1/4 Teaspoon thyme or basil
- As Needed olive oil

Steps

1. Line a rimmed baking sheet with parchment paper.

2. When ready to cook, set Pit Boss temperature to 225°F and preheat, lid closed for 15 minutes.

Grill: 225°

3. Remove the stem end from each tomato and cut the tomatoes into 1/2 inch thick slices.

4. Combine the salt, pepper, sugar, and thyme or basil in a small bowl and mix.

5. Pour olive oil into the well of a dinner plate.

6. Dip one side of each tomato slice in the olive oil and arrange on the baking sheet. Dust the tomato slices with the seasoning mixture.

7. Arrange the pan directly on the grill grate and roast the tomatoes until the juices stop running and the edges have contracted about 3 hours. Remove from grill and enjoy it!

6. BURNT ORANGE JULEP COCKTAIL

Prep Time : 5 Minutes

Cook Time : 1 hour

Pellets : Maple

This one's all about the bitters and bourbon. Refresh your taste buds with this fragrant citrus cocktail. Burnt orange agave, mint and the perfect amount of bourbon make for a cocktail you'll be buzzing over.

How Many People Are You Serving? 1

Ingredients

- 1 orange
- As Needed brown sugar
- 3/4 Ounce agave
- 1 Bunch mint
- 2 Ounce bourbon
- 2 Dash Angostura orange bitters

Steps

1. When ready to cook, set Pit Boss temperature to 500°F and preheat, lid closed for 15 minutes. Grill: 500°

2. Candied oranges: Slice orange into wheels and fully coat in brown sugar. Grill: 500°

3. Place directly on the grill grate and cook 15 minutes each side until grill marks develop. Remove wheels from the grill, set aside, and cool. Reserve 2 wheels for garnish. Grill: 500°

4. To make the burnt orange agave: Reduce the grill temperature to 200°F. In a small pan, combine the candied oranges in a thinned-out agave syrup (25% water added to agave syrup) and place directly on the grill grate. Cook 30-45 minutes or to taste. 1 orange slice per ounce of syrup made. Grill: 200°

5. To mix the cocktail: Add burnt orange agave and 5-6 mint leaves into a mixing tin. Muddle ingredients to release oils of mint.

6. Add bourbon, bitters, crushed ice, and shake lightly. Pour all contents into a glass or copper mug and add more crushed ice.

7. Garnish with candied orange wheel and mint. Enjoy!

7. BLACKBERRY BOURBON SMASH

Prep Time : 5 Minutes

Cook Time : 10 Minutes

Pellets : Apple

Blackberries, thyme leaves, and grilled limes give this bourbon drink an infusion of wood-fired flavor.

How Many People Are You Serving? 8

Ingredients

- ❖ 8 limes, halved
- ❖ 1/3 cup sugar
- ❖ 12 Ounce blackberries
- ❖ 2 Sprig thyme
- ❖ 1 Cup Pit Boss Smoked Simple Syrup
- ❖ 1 Quart soda water
- ❖ 2 Ounce bourbon

Steps

1. When ready to cook, set Pit Boss temperature to 500°F and preheat, lid closed, for 10 to 15 minutes. Grill: 500°

2. Dip cut side of limes in granulated sugar and place directly on the grill grate cut side down. Grill 10 minutes or until grill marks develop. Grill: 500°

3. Remove from grill and let cool. When cool enough to handle, juice limes and reserve.

4. Combine the blackberries with 2 Tbsp sugar. Using the rim of a glass or a fork, lightly crush the blackberries to allow some of the juice to escape.

5. Add 2 sprigs of thyme. Allow the blackberries to sit in the sugar for 30 minutes. Remove the thyme sprigs.

6. Combine the lime juice and Pit Boss Simple Syrup. Stir in the crushed blackberries. Add 3 cups of the club soda and stir.

7. Taste, adding more club soda if desired. This mixture can be served as a non-alcoholic drink.

8. To make the Blackberry Smash, fill a Collins glass with ice. Pour in 1/2 cup of the blackberry-limeade, then 2 oz of your favorite bourbon.

9. Stir to mix and garnish with a thyme sprig. Enjoy!

8. GRILLED WATERMELON

Prep Time : 30 Minutes

Cook Time : 10 Minutes

Pellets : Cherry

This grilled fruit recipe is a sure-fire way to impress every last guest at your neighborhood BBQ.

How Many People Are You Serving? 4

Ingredients

- ❖ 8 Slices seedless watermelon

- To Taste sea salt
- 2 Tablespoon honey

Steps

1. Lightly sprinkle the watermelon wedges on both sides with salt.

2. Stand the watermelon wedges on their edges on a rack over a sink or pan and let them drain for half an hour.

3. When ready to cook, set Pit Boss temperature to 500°F and preheat, lid closed for 15 minutes. Grill: 500°

4. After the watermelon has drained, rinse each piece under cold running water. Place each piece between two folded paper towels and gently but firmly press to remove excess water.

5. Brush the watermelon lightly on both sides with the honey.

6. Place the watermelon slices on the grill grate and Pit Boss them until grill marks have formed and the melon is slightly softened about 5 minutes. Grill: 500°

7. Remove from grill and sprinkle with sea salt and squeeze fresh lime juice over the top. Enjoy!

9. SMOKED SHREDDED BRUSSELS SPROUT SALAD

Prep Time : 20 Minutes

Cook Time : 30 Minutes

Pellets : Hickory

Roasted parsnips, shallots, and sweet potatoes are combined with shaved brussels sprouts, then get tossed with a block of goat cheese, orange juice, and champagne vinegar dressing for a smoky, wood-fired salad.

How Many People Are You Serving? 6

Ingredients

- 1 sweet potato, peeled and cut into 1/2 inch cubes
- 2 parsnips, peeled and cut 1/2 inch thick on the bias
- 4 shallots, sliced 1/4 inch thick
- 4 Tablespoon olive oil
- As Needed kosher salt
- As Needed freshly ground black pepper
- 2 oranges, halved
- 4 Ounce crumbled goat cheese
- 2 Tablespoon champagne vinegar
- 1 Pound Brussels sprouts, shaved
- 3/4 cup pomegranate seeds
- 3 Tablespoon fresh chopped mint

Steps

1. When ready to cook, set Pit Boss temperature to 450°F and preheat, lid closed for 15 minutes. Grill: 500°

2. Combine the sweet potato, parsnips, shallots, and 2 tablespoons of olive oil on a baking sheet, season with salt and pepper, and toss to coat. Spread out in a single layer. Place the baking sheet on the grill and roast until the vegetables are golden and beginning to crisp about 30 minutes. Transfer to a wire rack and let cool to room temperature.

3. While the vegetables cook, place the oranges cut side down on the grill and cook until soft and slightly browned, about 15

minutes. Remove from the grill, allow to cool and then squeeze the juice into a measuring cup, reserving 5 tablespoons of it for the vinaigrette. Grill: 500°

4. For the Vinaigrette: In a blender or food processor, mix the goat cheese, 5 tablespoons of orange juice, and the vinegar until smooth. On low speed, pour in the remaining 2 tablespoons of oil, blending until combined. Season with salt and pepper to taste.

5. Combine the shaved Brussels sprouts and roasted vegetables in a large bowl. Pour the vinaigrette over the salad and toss to coat. Taste, adding more salt as desired. Sprinkle with the pomegranate seeds and the mint to garnish. Enjoy!

10. SMOKED PICO DE GALLO

Prep Time : 10 Minutes

Cook Time : 30 Minutes

Pellets : Mesquite

Who knew smoked tomatoes would be so amazing? Chef Timothy did. Pair it with just about anything. Hell, put it on cardboard and you'll have a winner. It's that good.

How Many People Are You Serving? 4

Ingredients

- 3 cup diced Roma tomatoes
- 1 jalapeño, diced
- 1/2 red onion, diced
- 1/2 bunch cilantro, finely chopped
- 2 lime, juiced
- To Taste salt
- To Taste olive oil

Steps

1. When ready to cook, set Pit Boss temperature to 180°F and preheat, lid closed for 15 minutes. For optimal flavor, use Super Smoke if available. Grill: 180°

2. Place the diced tomatoes on a small sheet pan spreading them into a thin layer. Place the sheet pan directly on the grill and smoke for 30 minutes. Grill: 180°

3. When the tomatoes are finished, toss all ingredients in a medium bowl and finish with lime juice, salt, and olive oil to taste. Serve and enjoy!

11. GRILLED WINTER CHOP SALAD

Prep Time : 20 Minutes

Cook Time : 10 Minutes

Pellets : Hickory

Grilled radicchio and endive lettuce, toasted almonds, salami, and provolone cheese combined with a grilled lemon vinaigrette for a colorfully fresh chopped winter salad.

How Many People Are You Serving? 4

Ingredients

- ❖ 2 Head radicchio, quartered
- ❖ 2 Head endive, chopped
- ❖ 2 Head endive, chopped
- ❖ As Needed olive oil
- ❖ As Needed kosher salt
- ❖ As Needed freshly ground black pepper
- ❖ 2 Whole lemons, halved
- ❖ 1/2 coarsely chopped almonds
- ❖ 1 Small shallot, finely diced
- ❖ 1/4 Cup red wine vinegar
- ❖ 1 Teaspoon salt
- ❖ 1/2 Cup olive oil
- ❖ 1/2 Teaspoon freshly ground black pepper
- ❖ 1 (5-1/2 oz) log salami, diced into 1/2 inch pieces
- ❖ 1/2 Cup diced provolone cheese
- ❖ 4 Whole fire-roasted red peppers, drained and cut into thin strips
- ❖ 1 pear or apple, diced into 1/2 inch pieces

Steps

1. When ready to cook, set Pit Boss temperature to 375°F and preheat, lid closed for 15 minutes. Grill: 375°

2. Drizzle the radicchio and endive with olive oil and season with salt and pepper.

3. When the grill is up to temperature, add the lettuces and cook with the lid closed for 2 to 4 minutes per side, until they begin to wilt. Remove from the grill. Grill: 375°

4. Drizzle halved lemons with olive oil and place cut-side down on the grill for 2 to 3 minutes. Grill: 375°

5. In an oven-proof skillet, add the almonds to the grill. Close the lid and toast for 2 to 3 minutes. Remove from the grill. Grill: 375°

6. To Make the Vinaigrette: Combine shallots, red wine vinegar, and the grilled lemon juice in a bowl and add salt. While whisking the red wine vinegar mixture, slowly pour in olive oil until combined. Add black pepper.

7. Chop the grilled lettuces into bite-sized pieces and arrange in a bowl. Top with endive, salami, provolone, peppers, pears, and toasted almonds. Toss with vinaigrette and season with salt and pepper to taste. Enjoy!

12. GRILLED BROCCOLI RABE

Prep Time : 15 Minutes

Cook Time : 10 Minutes

Pellets : Cherry

A close relative of broccoli, broccoli rabe, or rapini is lightly seasoned with sea salt, olive oil, and lemon for a vegetable dish worthy of the main course.

How Many People Are You Serving? 4

Ingredients

- 4 Tablespoon extra-virgin olive oil
- 4 Bunch broccoli rabe or broccolini
- To Taste kosher salt
- 1 lemon, halved

Steps

1. When ready to cook, set Pit Boss temperature to 450°F and preheat, lid closed for 15 minutes.

Grill: 450°

2. On a platter or in a mixing bowl, drizzle the olive oil over the broccoli rabe. Use your hands to mix thoroughly, coating the vegetables evenly with the oil. Season with sea salt.

3. Place the broccoli rabe in one layer directly on the lowest grill grate. Close the lid and cook for 5 to 10 minutes. You want there to be some color and slight char on the first side. Flip and cook for a few more minutes.

Grill: 450°

4. Transfer the broccoli rabe to a serving platter and squeeze the juice of half a lemon evenly over the top.

5. Serve with more lemon wedges on the side. Enjoy!

13. GRILLED BABY CARROTS AND FENNEL WITH ROMESCO

Prep Time : 15 Minutes

Cook Time : 45 Minutes

Pellets : Oak

Smoked romesco sauce on top of this roasted trio of baby carrots, fingerling potatoes, and fennel bulbs will make you sing Hallelujah thanks to it intensely fresh and tangy wood-fired flavor.

How Many People Are You Serving? 8

Ingredients

- 1 Pound slender rainbow carrots or regular carrots with tops on
- 2 fennel bulbs, stalks, and cores removed and halved
- 1 Pound fingerling potatoes, washed and halved lengthwise
- 1/4 Cup olive oil
- kosher salt
- 1 Tablespoon thyme or rosemary leaves

Steps

1. When ready to cook, set Pit Boss temperature to 500°F and preheat, lid closed for 15 minutes.

Grill: 500°

2. Trim the carrot tops to 1 inch. Peel the carrots and halve any larger ones so they are all about 1/2 inch thick. Cut the fennel bulbs lengthwise into 1/2 inch thick slices. Place the carrots, fennel, and potato slices in a large mixing bowl. Drizzle with olive oil and a generous teaspoon of salt. Toss to coat the vegetables evenly with the oil.

3. Transfer the vegetables to a sheet pan. Nestle a few sprigs of herbs into the vegetables as well.

4. Place the pan directly on the grill grate and cook, stirring occasionally until the vegetables are browned and softened, about 35 to 45 minutes. Allow to cool and serve with the Smoked Romesco Sauce. Enjoy!

14. SMOKED COLD BREW COFFEE

Prep Time : 15 Minutes

Cook Time : 2 Hours

Pellets : Cherry

Add some mojo to your morning cup of Joe. Our smokin' recipe infuses cherrywood richness into your brew for the full-bodied flavor you'll keep coming back to.

How Many People Are You Serving? 8

Ingredients

- 12 Ounce coarse ground coffee
- To Taste heavy cream or milk
- To Taste sugar

Steps

1. Place half the coffee grounds in a plastic container and slowly pour 3-1/2 cups water over the top of the grounds. Add remaining grounds and pour another 3-1/2 cups water over the top in a circular motion.

2. Press the grounds down into the water using the back of a spoon. Cover and transfer to the refrigerator and let sit for 18 to 24 hours.

3. Remove from refrigerator and strain into a clean container through a fine-mesh strainer or double layer of cheesecloth.

4. When ready to cook, set Pit Boss temperature to 180°F and preheat, lid closed for 15 minutes. For optimal flavor, use Super Smoke if available.

5. Pour the cold brew into a shallow baking dish and place directly on the grill grate. Smoke for 1 to 2 hours depending on the desired level of smoke.

6. Remove from grill and place over an ice bath to cool. Drink as is over ice, with cream or sugar, or use in your favorite coffee recipes. Enjoy!

15. GRILLED CORN ON THE COB WITH PARMESAN AND GARLIC

Prep Time : 5 Minutes

Cook Time : 30 Minutes

Pellets : Mesquite

Give this summer side a cheesy garlic kick. Fresh corn is covered in a garlic butter mix, grilled till tender, and finished with melt-in-your-mouth parmesan and a parsley garnish.

How Many People Are You Serving? 6

Ingredients

- 4 Tablespoon butter, melted
- 2 Clove garlic, minced
- To Taste salt and pepper
- 8 ears fresh corn
- 1/2 Cup shaved Parmesan
- 1 Tablespoon chopped parsley

Steps

1. When ready to cook, set Pit Boss temperature to 450°F and preheat, lid closed for 15 minutes.

Grill: 450°

2. Place butter, garlic, salt, and pepper in a medium bowl and mix well.

3. Peel back corn husks and remove the silk. Rub corn with half of the garlic butter mixture.

4. Close husks and place directly on the grill grate. Cook for 25 to 30 minutes, turning occasionally until corn is tender.

Grill: 450°

5. Remove from grill, peel, and discard husks. Place corn on a serving tray, drizzle with remaining butter, and top with Parmesan and parsley.

16. SALT CRUSTED BAKED POTATOES

Prep Time : 15 Minutes

Cook Time : 1 hour

Pellets : Oak

Salty and crisp on the outside, warm and creamy on the inside. Finish these potatoes with a dollop of butter and your toppings of choice.

How Many People Are You Serving? 4

Ingredients

- 6 russet potatoes, scrubbed and dried
- 3 Tablespoon canola oil
- 1 Tablespoon kosher salt
- As Needed butter
- As Needed sour cream
- As Needed Chives, fresh
- As Needed Bacon Bits
- As Needed cheddar cheese

Steps

1. In a large bowl, coat the potatoes in canola oil and sprinkle heavily with salt.

2. When ready to cook, set Pit Boss temperature to 450°F and preheat, lid closed for 15 minutes.

Grill: 450°

3. Place the potatoes directly on the grill grate and bake for 30-40 minutes, or until soft in the middle when pricked with a fork. Serve loaded with your favorite toppings. Enjoy!

17. GRILLED SALMON W/ HONEY SRIRACHA LIME GLAZE

Ingredients

- 4 to 6 pieces of skinless salmon fillet, approximately 6 oz each
- 1/3 C olive oil
- ¼ C Grilla AP Rub
- ¼ C honey
- 2 TB lime juice
- 2 TB Sriracha

Directions

1. Use a paper towel to pat salmon dry. Brush fish with olive oil and dust with rub. Preheat Grilla Grill to 300 degrees.
2. Place fish on grill flat-side up. Once you have grill marks, flip the fish over. It should only take about 5 to 8 minutes per side. You can check for grill marks by lifting one corner of the fish with a spatula.
3. Be very gentle as the fish will become more delicate as it cooks.
4. Once you flip the fish, start brushing the glaze on.
5. Once the fish starts to feel firm and has grill marks on both sides, it is done. If you like your salmon more rare, feel free to pull it off the grill earlier. You don't want to overcook it, but the glaze will help salvage any drier parts.

18. GRILLED WINTER CHOP SALAD

Prep Time : 20 Minutes

Cook Time : 10 Minutes

Pellets : Hickory

Grilled radicchio and endive lettuce, toasted almonds, salami, and provolone cheese combined with a grilled lemon vinaigrette for a colorfully fresh chopped winter salad.

How Many People Are You Serving? 4

Ingredients

- 2 Head radicchio, quartered
- 2 Head endive, chopped
- 2 Head endive, chopped
- As Needed olive oil
- As Needed kosher salt
- As Needed freshly ground black pepper
- 2 Whole lemons, halved
- 1/2 coarsely chopped almonds
- 1 small shallot, finely diced
- 1/4 cup red wine vinegar
- 1 teaspoon salt
- 1/2 cup olive oil
- 1/2 teaspoon freshly ground black pepper
- 1 (5-1/2 oz) log salami, diced into 1/2 inch pieces
- 1/2 cup diced provolone cheese
- 4 Whole fire-roasted red peppers, drained and cut into thin strips
- 1 pear or apple, diced into 1/2 inch pieces

Steps

1. When ready to cook, set Pit Boss temperature to 375°F and preheat, lid closed for 15 minutes. Grill: 375°

2. Drizzle the radicchio and endive with olive oil and season with salt and pepper.

3. When the grill is up to temperature, add the lettuces and cook with the lid closed for 2 to 4 minutes per side, until they begin to wilt. Remove from the grill. Grill: 375°

4. Drizzle halved lemons with olive oil and place cut-side down on the grill for 2 to 3 minutes. Grill: 375°

5. In an oven-proof skillet, add the almonds to the grill. Close the lid and toast for 2 to 3 minutes. Remove from the grill. Grill: 375°

6. To Make the Vinaigrette: Combine shallots, red wine vinegar, and the grilled lemon juice in a bowl and add salt. While whisking the red wine vinegar mixture, slowly pour in olive oil until combined. Add black pepper.

7. Chop the grilled lettuces into bite-sized pieces and arrange in a bowl. Top with endive, salami, provolone, peppers, pears, and toasted almonds. Toss with vinaigrette and season with salt and pepper to taste. Enjoy!

19. LEMON & GARLIC ASPARAGUS

Cooking Time: 2 Hours

Yield: 2 Servings

The Heat: Hardwood Apple

Ingredients

- 2 cups of asparagus
- Olive oil, for greasing
- Salt and pepper, to taste
- 4 tablespoons of butter
- 4 garlic cloves, minced
- 1 lemon, zest

Directions

1. Preheat the electric smoker grill for 20 minutes at 200 degrees F.

2. Put the trimmed asparagus in boiling water for one minute.

3. Take out the asparagus and pat dry with a paper towel.

4. Sprinkle the vegetables with salt, pepper, and oil.

5. Melt butter along with garlic, and lemon zest in the microwave and pour over the asparagus

6. Transfer the asparagus to aluminum foil pan.

7. Put a pan on the grill grate and set the temperature of the electric smoker to 225 degrees F.

8. Cook the asparagus for 2 hours.

9. Once the asparagus is cooked, it to the serving plate and serve.

20. CRAB STUFFED MUSHROOMS

Cook Time: 4-6 hour

Prep Time: 15 Mins

Ingredients

- 1 package cream cheese, softened
- 1/2 (2 oz) package imitation crab, chopped
- 1 tablespoon lemon, juice
- 2 teaspoon lemon, zest
- 3/4 cup panko japanese bread crumbs
- 1/2 cup divided parmesan cheese, shredded
- 2 tablespoon parsley, fresh
- 1 teaspoon pit boss chop house steak rub
- 12 porcini mushroom caps, cleaned and destemmed

Directions:

- In a large bowl, combine the cream cheese, imitation crab, breadcrumbs, ¼ cup of the parmesan cheese, lemon zest, lemon juice, parsley, and Pit Boss Chophouse Steak seasoning. Mix until thoroughly combined.

- Using a spoon, stuff a sizeable rounded tablespoon of the filling into the mushroom caps and gently pack it into the mushroom. Once all the mushrooms are stuffed, top with the remaining ¼ cup of parmesan cheese.

- Preheat your Pit Boss grill to 350F. Place the mushrooms onto a grill basket and grill for 5 minutes until the cheese is bubbly and golden and the mushrooms are tender.

- Serve while hot and enjoy!

21. LEMON-GARLIC GREEN BEANS

Cook Time: 20 Mins

Prep Time: 10 Mins

Ingredients

- 3 - 5 tbs butter
- 3 garlic, cloves
- 1 lb green bean, whole
- Pepper
- Pit boss lemon pepper garlic seasoning
- Salt

Directions:

- Turn your grill to smoke. Once the firepot catches - preheat your grill to 350° F.
- Melt the butter in a ramekin.
- While your grill is heating, line the grilling basket with tinfoil. Add the green beans and melted butter.
- Add salt, pepper, and Pit Boss Grills Lemon Pepper Garlic Seasoning to taste

- Add 2-3 cloves of minced garlic.

- Toss all ingredients until evenly mixed.

- Place basket on the grill and cook for 15-20 minutes. Toss the basket halfway through the cooking time.

- Once your lemon garlic green beans are finished, remove them and add them to a serving dish – contents are hot! Caution as the butter may boil, splatter a bit.

22. SPINACH ARTICHOKE CHICKEN GRILLED CHEESE

Cook Time: 20 Mins

Prep Time: 15 Mins

Ingredients

- 1/2 jar marinated artichoke hearts, drained and chopped
- 4 bread, slices
- 2 tablespoon butter, unsalted
- 2 chicken breast, raw
- 4 oz cream cheese, softened
- 1/4 cup parmesan cheese, shredded
- 1 tablespoon pit boss champion chicken seasoning, divided
- 1 bag spinach, fresh

Directions:

- Preheat your Pit Boss grill to 350F. Using one tablespoon of the Pit Boss Champion Chicken seasoning, season both chicken breasts. When the grill is up to temperature, grill chicken breasts until fully cooked, about 7 minutes on each side, remove from the grill, allow to cool and slice into bite-sized strips.

- In a large bowl, combine the cream cheese, spinach, artichoke hearts, parmesan cheese, and remaining Champion Chicken seasoning. Mix well until everything is thoroughly combined.

- On a stovetop, heat a large frypan over medium heat and add the butter. Spread the spinach artichoke mixture onto the bread, add the chicken, and cook until the bread is a deep golden brown and the cheese is melty.

- Remove from the pan and enjoy!

23. MEXICAN STREET CORN SALAD

Cook Time: 10 Mins

Prep Time: 10 Mins

Ingredients

- 1 tablespoon of chopped cilantro
- 4 corn, cob
- 1/2 cup crumbled feta cheese
- 1 lime, juiced
- 2 tablespoon mayo
- 1 teaspoon paprika, smoked
- 1 tablespoon pit boss champion chicken seasoning
- 1/4 cup sour cream

Directions:

- Preheat your Pit Boss Grill to 350F. Grill the corn cobs until slightly charred on all sides, about 10 minutes. Remove from the grill and allow to cool.
- Remove the kernels of corn from the cob and set them aside. In a separate bowl, mix the sour cream, mayonnaise,

lime juice, Champion Chicken seasoning, smoked paprika, and cilantro until smooth. Mix with the corn and feta cheese, then serve immediately.

24. BRUSSELS SPROUT SLAW WITH APPLE BUTTER DRESSING

Cook Time: 10 Mins

Prep Time: 40 Mins

Ingredients

- 1/4 cup (for apple butter dressing) apple butter
- 2 tablespoon (for apple butter dressing) apple cider vinegar
- 8 (for the slaw) bacon, strip

- 2 lbs (for the slaw) brussels sprouts, rinsed, and trimmed
- 1/2 teaspoon (for apple butter dressing) chipotle pepper, ground
- 1 teaspoon (for apple butter dressing) cinnamon, ground
- 1/2 teaspoon (for apple butter dressing) coriander, ground
- 1 cup (for apple butter dressing) olive oil
- 1 (for apple butter dressing) orange, zest
- 1/2 cup (for the slaw) parmesan cheese, shredded
- 1/2 cup (for the slaw) pecans, toasted
- 1 teaspoon (for apple butter dressing) pit boss applewood smoked bacon seasoning
- 1/4 cup (for the slaw) pomegranate arils
- 1 (for the slaw) yellow onion
- Yellow onion, sliced

Directions:

- **For The Slaw:** In a food processor, fit the bowl with a medium grating blade. Shred the brussels sprouts and set them aside. Place the bacon and yellow on a grill basket and season both sides with Pit Boss Applewood Smoked

Bacon Seasoning. Turn your Pit Boss Grill to 350F and grill for 5-10 minutes, or until bacon is crispy and the yellow onion is soft. Remove from grill and chop into ¼ inch pieces. Set aside.

- **For The Dressing:** in a large bowl, whisk together the oil, apple butter, coriander, chipotle pepper, cinnamon, vinegar, orange zest, and Applewood Smoked Bacon seasoning. Whisk to combine.

- **To Assemble The Salad:** In a large salad bowl, stir together the shredded Brussels sprouts, chopped pecans, chopped bacon, parmesan cheese, pomegranate arils, and dressing. Serve and enjoy!

25. GREEN CHILE MASHED POTATOES

Cook Time: 40 Mins

Prep Time: 20 Mins

Ingredients

- 1 stick butter, unsalted
- 1 can green chiles, drained
- 1/4 - 1/2 warm milk, whole
- Pit boss competition smoked rub
- 2 tablespoon pit boss competition smoked seasoning
- 3 lbs russet potatoes, peeled and cut (large chunks)

Directions:

- **For The Mashed Potatoes:** Add the potatoes to a large pot and add enough cold water to cover them. Bring to a simmer over medium heat until the potatoes are tender enough to be pierced with a fork, about 30-35 minutes. Drain the potatoes.

- Add the potatoes to a large mixing bowl. Add the butter, Competition Smoked Seasoning, drained green chiles, and ¼ cup of warm milk. Mash until smooth and lump-free. If potatoes are too thick, add more milk, a tablespoon at a time, until you reach your desired consistency.

- Serve and enjoy!

26. SMOKED SCALLOPED POTATOES

Cook Time: 60 Mins

Prep Time: 30 Mins

Ingredients

- 1 stick of butter
- Cast iron skillet or pan
- 1/2 cheddar jack or colby jack cheese, shredded
- Medium yellow onion
- Pit boss bacon cheddar seasoning
- 6-8 potatoes
- Salt and pepper
- Smoked guoda cheese, sliced

Directions:

- Preheat Grill to 350°F.
- Peel 6-8 potatoes and slice into 1/4 round slices, cover with water in a pot, and bring to boil, allow to boil for 2-3 minutes.

- In the cast-iron skillet, start to layer the potatoes and cheese. Starting by using a slotted spoon to remove potatoes from water. You will want some of the water from the boiling process to make it into the skillet, but not an excessive amount. Using a slotted spoon but not shaking the dry potatoes works perfectly.

- Once you have a base layer of potatoes, add a layer of sliced onion (approx. ½ of a medium yellow onion), salt, pepper, Pit Boss Bacon Cheddar Burger Seasoning, a drizzle of sweetened condensed milk, half a stick of butter cut into pats, and a layer of sliced smoked gouda cheese.

- Repeat on the 2nd layer. Top with grated cheddar jack or Colby jack cheese.

- Cook at 325°F-350°F for approx. One hour or until the potatoes are tender.

- For crustier cheese on top, turn the grill up to 425°F for the last 10 to 15 minutes or until the cheese is golden brown.

27. SOUTHERN GREEN BEANS

Cook Time: 60 mins

Prep Time: 15 mins

Ingredients

- 1 tablespoon butter, unsalted
- 2 cups chicken broth
- 2 pounds green beans, ends snapped off and longer beans snapped in half
- Hickory bacon seasoning
- 4 slices bacon, raw
- 2 cups water

Directions:

- Fire up your Pit Boss grill and set the temperature to 350°F. If you're using a gas or charcoal grill, set it up for medium heat. Place a cast-iron pan on the grill to preheat. Once the pan finishes preheating, place the four slices of bacon in the pan and cook for 15 minutes until the bacon has rendered and is crispy.

- Remove the bacon from the pan and reserve for later. Leave the pan and drippings on the grill, and add the green beans, chicken broth, water, and Hickory Bacon seasoning to taste. Close the lid on the grill and cook for an hour or until the beans are tender.

- Chop the bacon on a cutting board and mix it into the beans with the butter. Allow the beans to cook for another minute, then remove from the heat and serve.

28. GLUTEN FREE MASHED POTATO CAKES

Cook Time: 10 mins

Prep Time: 40 mins

Ingredients

- 1/2 cup bacon bits
- 2 tbsp butter
- 1 cup cheddar jack cheese, shredded
- 1 egg, whisked
- 1/3 cup flour, gluten free

- 3 cups mashed potatoes, prepared
- 1 tsp pit boss hickory bacon rub
- 4 scallions, minced
- 2 tsp spicy mustard

Directions:

- In a mixing bowl, combine mashed potatoes, bacon bits, scallions, mustard, cheddar jack cheese, and beaten egg. In a separate bowl, whisk together flour and a teaspoon of Pit Boss Hickory Bacon Rub. Incorporate dry into wet ingredients. Cover and refrigerate for 30 minutes.

- Remove mixture from the refrigerator, then divide into 12 balls (about 2 ½ inches in diameter), and set on a greased sheet tray. Use the bottom of a bowl to press down each potato ball to form a ½ inch thick patty. Season with an additional sprinkling of Hickory Bacon and set aside. Fire up your Pit Boss Platinum Series KC Combo or Pit Boss Griddle and preheat the grill to medium-low flame. If using a gas or charcoal grill, preheat a cast-iron skillet over medium-low heat.

- Add butter and oil to the grill to melt, then place mashed potato cakes on the grill. Cook for 2 to 3 minutes per side until golden brown.

- Remove from the grill. Serve warm with sour cream, reserved bacon bits, and scallions.

29. CHILI VERDE SAUCE

Cook Time: 10 mins

Prep Time: 15 mins

Ingredients

- 1 cup cilantro
- 3 cloves garlic, peeled
- 1 medium onion, peeled and quartered
- ¼ cup olive oil
- 3-4 serrano chili pepper, halved and seeded
- 1 tbsp sweet heat rub
- 1 lb. Tomatillos, husks removed

Directions:

- Fire up your pellet grill and set the temperature to 350°F. If you're using a gas or charcoal grill, set it up for medium-high heat. In a bowl, toss the tomatillos, onion, garlic, and peppers with the oil and toss to coat evenly.

- Grill vegetables until a little charred and bubbling on all sides, about 10 – 20 minutes. Remove from grill and allow to cool slightly.

- Transfer grilled vegetables to a blender and add the cilantro, lime juice, olive oil, and Sweet Heat Rub. Pulse the ingredients until they have a consistent texture to them.

30. SMOKED PAPRIKA CAULIFLOWER

Cooking Time: 2 Hours

Yield: 4 Servings

The Heat: Hardwood Apple

Ingredients

. 1 large head of Cauliflower, cut into florets

- 6 tablespoons olive oil
- 1 tablespoon white pepper
- 1 teaspoon of smoked paprika

Directions

1. Preheat the smoker grill for 220 degrees F.

2. In a mixing bowl, add olive oil, paprika, pepper and cauliflower.

3. Toss ingredients well.

4. Smoke cauliflower for 2 hours.

5. Once done, serve.

31. ROASTED SWEET POTATO STEAK FRIES

Prep Time : 10 Minutes

Cook Time : 40 Minutes

Pellets : Hickory

These hickory roasted sweet potato fries will blow you away. Thick-cut sweet potatoes are given a smokin' kick with fresh rosemary for the perfect savory sidekick for any meal.

How Many People Are You Serving? 4

Ingredients

- 3 Whole sweet potatoes
- 4 Tablespoon extra-virgin olive oil
- To Taste salt and pepper
- 2 tablespoon fresh chopped rosemary

Steps

1. When ready to cook, set Pit Boss temperature to 450°F and preheat, lid closed for 15 minutes. Grill: 450°

2. Cut sweet potatoes into wedges and toss with olive oil, salt, pepper, and rosemary. Spread on a parchment-lined baking sheet and put it in the grill. Cook for 15 minutes then flip and continue to cook until lightly browned and cooked through about 40 to 45 minutes total. Grill: 450°

3. Serve with your favorite dipping sauce. Grill: 450°

32. SMOKED CABBAGE

Cooking Time: 2 Hours

Yield: 2 Servings

The Heat: Hardwood Apple

Ingredients

- 2 large cups of red cabbage
- 3 tablespoons of steak seasoning
. 1 stick butter
- 1 vegetable bouillon cube

Directions

1. Preheat the electric smoker for 20 minutes at 250 degrees F.

2. Place the cabbage onto the tin foil pan and add butter.

3. Sprinkle vegetable bouillon cubes and then season it with steak seasoning.

4. Wrap the tin foil leaving the top slightly open.

5. Cook on the grill grate for 2 hours at 200 degrees F.

6. Once done, serve

33. EGGPLANT

Cooking Time: 1 Hour

Yield: 6 Servings

The Heat: Hardwood Apple

Ingredient

- 4 cloves of garlic, minced
- 2 tablespoons of balsamic vinegar
- Salt and pepper, to taste
- 6 eggplants
- 6 tablespoons of olive oil

Directions

1. Preheat the smoker for 50 minutes at 220 degrees F.

2. Cut the eggplant in circles.

3. Marinate the eggplant in garlic, pepper, salt, vinegar, and olive oil mixture.

4. After one hour, place the eggplant onto smoker grill, and a smoker for 60 minutes.

34. GRILLED BROCCOLI RABE

Prep Time : 15 Minutes

Cook Time : 10 Minutes

Pellets : Cherry

A close relative of broccoli, broccoli rabe, or rapini is lightly seasoned with sea salt, olive oil, and lemon for a vegetable dish worthy of the main course.

How Many People Are You Serving? 4

Ingredients

- 4 Tablespoon extra-virgin olive oil
- 4 Bunch broccoli rabe or broccolini
- To Taste kosher salt

- 1 lemon, halved

Steps

1. When ready to cook, set Pit Boss temperature to 450°F and preheat, lid closed for 15 minutes. Grill: 450°

2. On a platter or in a mixing bowl, drizzle the olive oil over the broccoli rabe. Use your hands to mix thoroughly, coating the vegetables evenly with the oil. Season with sea salt.

3. Place the broccoli rabe in one layer directly on the lowest grill grate. Close the lid and cook for 5 to 10 minutes. You want there to be some color and slight char on the first side. Flip and cook for a few more minutes.

Grill: 450°

4. Transfer the broccoli rabe to a serving platter and squeeze the juice of half a lemon evenly over the top.

5. Serve with more lemon wedges on the side. Enjoy!

35. SMOKED PUMPKIN SOUP

Prep Time : 15 Minutes

Cook Time : 2 Hours

Pellets : Alder

Smoke that pumpkin into a warm-bellied soup that's smoldering with fall spices. Serve it up on a chilly evening--it's fall food at it's best.

How Many People Are You Serving? 6

Ingredients

- ❖ 5 Pound Pumpkin, whole
- ❖ 3 Tablespoon butter
- ❖ 1 onion, diced

- 2 Clove garlic, minced
- 1 Tablespoon brown sugar
- 1 teaspoon paprika
- 1/4 teaspoon ground cinnamon
- 1/8 teaspoon ground nutmeg
- 1/8 teaspoon ground allspice
- 1/2 cup apple cider
- 5 cup chicken broth
- 1/2 cup whipped cream
- As Needed fresh parsley

Steps

1. Using a sturdy knife, cut the pumpkin into quarters. Scoop out the seeds and stringy fibers. Separate the seeds from the fibers, and save the seeds for roasting, if desired.

2. When ready to cook, start the Pit Boss grill and set the temperature to 165F with the lid closed.

3. Arrange the pumpkin quarters, skin-side down, directly on the grill grate. Smoke for 1 hour. Grill: 165°

4. Increase the temperature to 300F and roast the pumpkin until it is tender and can easily be pierced with a fork, about 90 minutes. Let cool, then separate the pumpkin flesh from the skin. Grill: 300°

5. Meanwhile, melt the butter over medium heat in a 4-quart saucepan or stockpot.

6. Saute the onion and garlic until soft and translucent, about 5 minutes.

7. Stir in the brown sugar, smoked paprika, cinnamon, nutmeg, and allspice. Immediately add the apple cider, and cook for several minutes until the mixture is reduced and syrupy.

8. Add the pumpkin and chicken broth. Let the soup simmer for 20 to 30 minutes.

9. Using a blender or hand-held immersion blender, blend the soup until it is smooth. Add salt and pepper to taste. If it is too thick, stir in more chicken broth.

10. Divide the soup into bowls and drizzle with the heavy cream. Top with a sprig of parsley, if desired.

36. BAKED DEEP DISH SUPREME PIZZA

Prep Time : 15 Minutes

Cook Time : 30 MINUTES

Pellets : Apple

This Deep Dish Supreme Pizza is loaded with pepperoni, sausage, onions, and peppers, topped with mozzarella cheese, and baked in a cast-iron skillet on the grill.

How Many People Are You Serving? 4

Ingredients

- As Needed extra-virgin olive oil
- Ounce pizza dough
- 1/2 cup pizza sauce
- 2 cup mozzarella cheese

- To Taste Parmesan cheese
- 1 Teaspoon fresh oregano
- 1 Teaspoon fresh basil
- Pound Mild Italian Sausage
- 1 Half Bell Pepper, Green
- 2 Tablespoon onion, diced
- 1 Half Bell Pepper, Red
- To Taste Mushrooms, fresh
- To Taste Pepperoni, sliced
- To Taste black olives

Steps

1. When ready to cook, set grill temperature to High and preheat, lid closed for 15 minutes.

2. Coat a 10 to the 12-inch cast-iron pan with extra virgin olive oil. Add your dough to the pan and press out through the bottom and up around the sides.

3. To assemble the pizza, spread sauce on top of the dough and add all toppings. Add mozzarella and freshly grated parmesan on top and sprinkle with oregano and basil.

4. Bake for 25-30 minutes or until the crust is golden brown and cheese and sauce is bubbling.

Grill: 450°

5. Let rest for 5-10 minutes before slicing. Enjoy!

37. BACON ONION RING

Prep Time : 10 Minutes

Cook Time : 1 hour

Pellets : Mesquite

These onion rings are wrapped in bacon & will kick any savory or spicy craving you've got.

How Many People Are You Serving? 6

Ingredients

- 16 Slices bacon
- 2 Whole Vidalia onion, sliced

- 1 Tablespoon Chili Garlic Sauce
- 1 Tablespoon yellow mustard
- 1 Teaspoon honey

Steps

1. Wrap a piece of bacon around an individual onion ring; continue until bacon is gone. Some onion slices may be larger and require 2 pieces of bacon to complete a ring.

2. Place a skewer through the bacon-wrapped onion slice, to keep bacon from unraveling while cooking.

3. When ready to cook, set the temperature to 400 degrees F and preheat, lid closed, for 10 to 15 minutes.

4. Meanwhile, mix chili garlic sauce and yellow mustard in a small bowl until incorporated; add honey.

5. Place skewers on the grill grate and cooks for approximately 90 minutes, flipping after 45 minutes. Enjoy!

Grill: 400°

38. ROASTED PEACH SALSA

Prep Time : 25 Minutes

Cook Time : 10 Minutes

Pellets : Cherry

Check out this fresh take on a summer standby. We grill peaches, tomatoes, and jalapeños and combine them with garlic, green onions, lime juice, and apple cider vinegar for a truly unique salsa.

How Many People Are You Serving? 6

Ingredients

- 6 Whole Peaches, fresh
- 3 Tomatoes, fresh
- 2 Whole jalapeño

- 2 Whole Onions, green
- 1/2 cup cilantro
- 2 Clove garlic
- 5 teaspoon apple cider vinegar
- 1 Teaspoon lime juice
- 1/2 teaspoon salt
- 1/4 teaspoon black pepper

Steps

1. When ready to cook, set the Pit Boss to 375°F and preheat, lid closed for 15 minutes.

2. Place the halved peaches, halved tomatoes, and whole jalapeños directly on the grill grate. Close the lid and roast for 8-10 minutes or until the skin has split and the tomatoes and jalapeños have blistered. Grill: 375°

3. Remove from grill and allow to cook until the fruit can be easily handled.

4. Remove the skin from the peaches and tomatoes. Remove the skin, stems, and seeds from the jalapeños.

5. Place peeled peaches, tomatoes, jalapeños, and green onions in a large food processor and pulse until coarsely chopped.

6. Add all other ingredients and pulse until desired consistency is reached. Use short pulses for chunky salsa or long pulses for smoother salsa.

7. Serve immediately or transfer to jars and chill until ready to serve. It Will lasts about 1 week in the refrigerator. Enjoy!

39. ROASTED GREEN BEANS WITH BACON

Prep Time : 15 Minutes

Cook Time : 20 Minutes

Pellets : Apple

Everything's better with bacon, and our roasted green beans recipe is no exception. This no-fuss recipe is a great side for any meal. Just toss all the ingredients together, lay them on a sheet pan & throw them on your grill. Doesn't get any easier or tastier.

How Many People Are You Serving? 4

Ingredients

- Pound Green Beans, fresh
- 4 Strips Bacon, Cut Into Small Pieces
- 4 Tablespoon extra-virgin olive oil

- 2 Clove garlic, minced
- 1 teaspoon kosher salt

Steps

1. When ready to cook, set grill temperature to High and preheat, lid closed for 15 minutes.

2. Toss all ingredients together and spread out evenly on a sheet tray.

3. Place the tray directly on the grill grate and roast until the bacon is crispy and beans are lightly browned about 20 minutes. Enjoy!

Grill: 450°

Lightning Source UK Ltd.
Milton Keynes UK
UKHW020755030621
384857UK00005B/144

9 781801 883955